Labour Defended against the Claims of Capital: Or the Unproductiveness of Capital proved with Reference to the Present Combinations amongst Journeymen
Thomas Hodgskin

Prism Key Press, 2013.
New York, NY.

www.PrismKeyPress.com

ISBN-13: 978-1490937779
ISBN-10: 1490937773

Labour Defended against the Claims of Capital: Or the Unproductiveness of Capital proved with Reference tothe Present Combinations amongst Journeymen

Thomas Hodgskin

TABLE OF CONTENTS

Note

Labour Defended Against the Claims of Capital

Note

IN all the debates on the law passed during the late session of Parliament, on account of the combinations of workmen, much stress is laid on the necessity of protecting capital. What capital performs is therefore a question of considerable importance, which the author was, on this account, induced to examine. As a result of this examination, it is his opinion that all the benefits attributed to capital arise from co-existing and skilled labour. He feels himself, on this account, called on to deny that capital has any just claim to the large share of the national produce now bestowed on it. This large share he has endeavoured to show is the cause of the poverty of the labourer; and he ventures to assert that the condition of the labourer can never be permanently improved till he can refute the theory, and is determined to oppose the practice of giving nearly everything to capital.

Labour Defended Against the Claims of Capital

Throughout this country at present there exists a serious contest between capital and labour. The journeymen of almost every trade have combined to obtain higher wages, and their employers have appealed to the legislature for protection. The contest is not only one of physical endurance, or who can stand out longest, but of argument and reason. It is possible for the workmen to force their masters into compliance, but they must convince the public of the justice of their demands. The press has, at present, a great influence over public questions; and by far the greater and more influential part of it is engaged on the side of the capitalist. Through it, however, and through public opinion, must the journeymen find their way to the legislature. They may possibly terrify their masters, but they can only obtain the support of any influential persons by an appeal to reason. To suggest some arguments in favour of labour against capital, is my chief motive for publishing the present pamphlet.

The labourers are very unfortunate, I conceive, in being surrounded by nations in a worse political condition than we are, and in some of which labour is still worse paid than here. Labourers are still more unfortunate in being descended from bondsmen and serfs. Personal slavery or villanage formerly existed in Britain, and all the living labourers still suffer from the bondage of their ancestors. Our claims are consequently never tried by the principles of justice. The law-giver and the capitalist always compare our wages with the wages of other labourers; and without adverting to what we produce, which seems the only criterion by which we ought to be paid, we are instantly condemned as insolent and ungrateful if we ask for more than was enjoyed by the slave of former times, and is now enjoyed by the half-starved slave of other countries.

By our increased skill and knowledge, labour is now probably ten times more productive than it was two hundred years ago; and we are, forsooth, to be contended with the same rewards which the bondsmen then received. All the advantages of our improvements go to the capitalist and the landlord. When, denied any share in our increased produce, we combine to obtain it, we are instantly threatened with summary punishment. New laws are fulminated against us, and if these are found insufficient we are threatened with laws still more severe.

Combination is of itself no crime; on the contrary, it is the principle on which societies are held together. When the Government supposes its existence threatened, or the country in danger, it calls on us all to combine for its protection. "Combinations of workmen," however, it says through Mr Huskisson, "must be put down." Frequently has it contracted alliances with other governments or made combinations to carry on war and shed blood; frequently has it called on the whole nation to combine when the object has been to plunder and massacre the unoffending subjects of some neighbouring state and frequently have such combinations had heaped on them all the epithets of the vocabulary of glory. No other combination seems unjust or mischievous, in the view of Government, but our combinations to obtain a proper reward for our labour. It is a heinous crime in the eyes of a legislature, composed exclusively of capitalists and landlords, and representing no other interests than their own, for us to try, by any means, to obtain for ourselves and for the comfortable subsistence of our families, a larger share of our own produce than these our masters choose to allow us. All the moral evils that ever plagued a society have been anticipated by the ministers from our persevering in our claims. To put down combinations they have departed from principles held sacred for upwards of two hundred years. They have made also a law handing us over to the magistrates like vagabonds and thieves, and we are to be condemned almost unheard, and without the privilege and formality of a public trial.

All that we are compelled to suffer, all that we have had inflicted on us, has been done for the advantage of capital. "Capital," says Mr Huskisson, "will be terrified out of the country, and the misguided workmen, unless they are stopped in time, will bring ruin on themselves and on us." "Capital," says the Marquis of Lansdowne, "must be protected. If its operations be not left free, if they are to be controlled by bodies of workmen, it will leave this for some more favoured country." Capital, if we believe these politicians, has improved England, and the want of capital is the cause of the poverty and sufferings of Ireland. Under the influence of such notions, no laws for the protection of capital are thought too severe, and few or no persons, except the labourers, see either impropriety or injustice in the fashionable mode of despising his claims, and laughing at his distresses.

In fact the legislature, the public at large, and especially our employers, decide on our claims solely by a reference to the former condition of the labourer, or to his condition in other countries. We are told to be contented, because we are not quite so badly off as the ragged Irish peasants who are suffering under a more grievous system even than the one which afflicts us. By them also we are destined to suffer; for they are imported here in crowds, and beat down the wages of our labour. We can have no hope, therefore, either of convincing the public or of calling the blush of shame into the cheek of those who are opulent by our toils, and who deride the poverty and sufferings they cause, by referring to the customs of any other society, either in times past or present. To obtain better treatment the labourers must appeal from practice to principle. We must put out of view how labour has been paid in times past, and how it is now paid in other countries, and we must show how it ought to be paid. This, I admit, is a difficult task, but the former condition of the labourer in this country, and his condition at present in other countries, leaving us no criterion to which we can or ought to appeal, we must endeavour to perform it.

The claims of capital, are, I am aware, sanctioned by almost universal custom; and as long as the labourer did not feel himself aggrieved by them, it was of no use opposing them with arguments. But now, when the practice excites resistance, we are bound, if possible, to overthrow the theory on which it is founded and justified. It is accordingly against this theory that my arguments will be directed. When we have settled the question, however, as to the claims of capital or labour, we shall have proceeded only one step towards ascertaining what ought now to be the wages of labour. The other parts of the inquiry will, I trust, be entered into by some of my fellow-labourers, and I shall content myself at present with examining the claims of the capitalists, as supported by the theories of political economy.

I admit that the subject is somewhat abstruse, but there is a necessity for the labourers to comprehend and be able to refute the received notions of the nature and utility of capital. Wages vary inversely as profits; or wages rise when profits fall, and profits rise when wages fall; and it is therefore profits, or the capitalist's share of the national produce, which is opposed to wages, or the share of the labourer. The theory on which profits are claimed, and which holds up capital, and accumulation of capital to our administration as the mainspring of human improvement, is that which I say the labourers must, in their own interest, examine, and must, before they can have any hope of a permanent improvement in their own conditions, be able to refute. They, indeed, are so satisfied that by their exertions all the wealth of society is produced that no doubt on the subject has ever entered their minds. This is not, however, the case with other people, and whenever the labourers claim larger wages, or combine to do themselves justice, they hear, both from the legislature and the Press, little or nothing about the necessity of rewarding labour, but much about the necessity of protecting capital. They must therefore be able to show the hollowness of the theory on which the claims of capital, and on which all the oppressive laws made for its protection are founded. This will, I hope, be a motive with them for endeavouring to comprehend the following observations, as it is my excuse for directing them, not so much to show what labour ought, as to what capital ought not to have.

"The produce of the earth," says Mr Ricardo — "All that is derived from its surface by the united application of labour, machinery and capital is divided among three classes of the community; namely, the proprietor of the land, the owner of the stock or capital necessary for its cultivation, and the labourers by whose industry it is cultivated." (Principles of Political Economy, Preface, p. 1, 2nd Ed.)

"It is self-evident," says Mr M'Culloch, "that only three classes, the labourers, the possessors of capital, and the proprietors of land, are ever directly concerned in the production of commodities. It is to them, therefore, that all which is derived from the surface of the earth, or from its bowels, by the united application of immediate labour, and of capital, or accumulated labour, must primarily belong. The other classes of society have no revenue except what they derive either voluntarily or by compulsion from these three classes."

The proportions in which the whole produce is divided among these three classes is said to be as follows: — "Land is of different degrees of fertility." "When, in the progress of society, land of the second quality (or an inferior degree of fertility to land before cultivated) is taken into cultivation, rent immediately commences on that of the first quality, and the amount of that rent will depend on the difference in the quality, and the amount of that rent will depend on the difference in the quality of these two portions or land." [Principles of Political Economy] Rent, therefore, or that quantity of the whole produce of the country which goes to the landlords, is, in every stage of society, that portion of this produce which is obtained from every district belonging to a politically organised nation, more than is obtained from the least fertile land cultivated by, or belonging to, that nation. It is the greater produce of all the land which is more fertile than the least fertile land cultivated. To produce this surplus would not break the back, and to give it up would not break the heart of the labourer. The landlord's share, therefore, does not keep the labourer poor.

The labourer's share of the produce of a country, according to this theory, is the "necessaries and conveniences required for the support of the labourer and his family; or that quantity which is necessary to enable the labourers, one with another, to subsist and to perpetuate their race, without either increase or diminution." Whatever may be the truth of the theory in other respects, there is no doubt of its correctness in this particular. The labourers do only receive, and ever have only received, as much as will subsist them, the landlords receive the surplus produce of the more fertile soils, and all the rest of the whole produce of labour in this and in every country goes to the capitalist under the name of profit for the use of his capital.

Capital which thus engrosses the whole produce of a country, except the bare subsistence of the labourer, and the surplus produce of fertile land, is, "the produce of labour," "is commodities," "is the food the labourer eats, and the machines he uses": so that we are obliged to give that enormous portion of the whole produce of the country which remains, after we have been supplied with subsistence, and the rent of the landlord has been paid, for the privilege of eating the food we have ourselves produced, and of using our own skill in producing more. Capital, the reader will suppose, must have some wonderful properties, when the labourer pays so exorbitantly for it. In fact, its claims are founded on its wonderful properties, and to them, therefore, I mean especially to direct his attention.

Several good and great men, whom we must all respect and esteem, seeing that capital did obtain all the large share I have mentioned, and being more willing, apparently, to defend and to explain the present order of society than to ascertain whether it could be improved, have endeavoured to point out the method in which capital aids production. From their writings I shall extract some passages explanatory of its effects. I must, however, beg not to be understood as doing this invidiously. The only motive I have for selecting these authors, as the representatives of the political economists, is, that they are by far the more efficient and eloquent supporters of the doctrine I do not assent to.

Mr M'Culloch says:

"The accumulation and employment of both fixed and circulating capital is indispensably necessary to elevate any nation in the scale of civilisation. And it is only by their conjoined and powerful operation that wealth can be largely produced and universally diffused." [Article "Political Economy" in Supplement to Encyclopedia Britannica.]

"The quantity of industry," he further says, "therefore not only increases in every country with the increase of the stock or capital which sets it in motion; but, in consequence of this increase, the division of labour becomes extended, new and more powerful implements and machines are invented, and the same quantity of labour is thus made to produce an infinitely greater quantity of commodities.

"Besides its effect in enabling labour to be divided, capital contributes to facilitate labour, and produce wealth in the three following ways:-

"First. — It enables us to execute work that could not be executed, or to produce commodities that could not be produced without it.

"Second. — It saves labour in the production of almost every species of commodities.

"Third. — It enables us to execute work better, as well as more expeditiously."

Mr Mill's account of these effects, though not so precise,

is still more astounding. "The labourer," he says, "has neither raw materials nor tools. These are provided for him by the capitalist. For making this provision the capitalist of course expects a reward." According to this statement, the capitalist provides for the labourer and only, therefore, expects a profit. In other parts of his book it is not the capitalist who provides, but the capital which works. He speaks of capital as an instrument of production co-operating with labour, as an active agent combining with labour to produce commodities, and thus he satisfies himself, and endeavours to prove to the reader that capital is entitled to all that large share of the produce it actually receives. He also attributes to capital power of accumulation. This power or tendency to accumulate, he adds, is not so great as the tendency of population to augment — and on the difference between these two tendencies he and other authors have erected a theory of society which places poor Mother Nature in no favourable light.

Without troubling myself to quote more passages from these authors, or to transcribe the opinion of other writers, I shall proceed to examine the effects of capital; and I shall begin with circulating capital. Mr M'Culloch says, "without circulating capital," meaning the food the labourer consumes, and the clothing he wears, "the labourer never could engage in any undertaking which did not yield an almost immediate return." Afterwards he says, "that division of labour is a consequence of previous accumulation of capital," and quotes the following passage from Dr Smith, as a proper expression for his own opinions:-

"Before labour can be divided, 'a stock of goods of different kinds must be stored up somewhere, sufficient to maintain the labourer, and to supply him with tools for carrying on his work. A weaver, for example, could not apply himself entirely to his peculiar business, unless there was beforehand stored up somewhere, either in his own possession, or in that of some other person, a stock sufficient for his maintenance, and for supplying him with the materials and implements required to carry on his work, till he has not only completed, but sold his web. This accumulation must evidently be previous to his applying himself for so long a time to a peculiar business.'"

The only advantage of circulating capital is that by it the labourer is enabled, he being assured of his present subsistence, to direct his power to the greatest advantage. He has time to learn an art, and his labour is rendered more productive when directed by skill. Being assured of immediate subsistence, he can ascertain which, with his peculiar knowledge and acquirements, and with reference to the wants of society, is the best method of labouring, and he can labour in this manner. Unless there were this assurance there could be no continuous thought, an invention, and no knowledge but that which would be necessary for the supply of our immediate animal wants. The weaver, I admit, could not complete his web, nor would the shipwright begin to build his ship, unless he knew that while he was engaged in this labour he should be able to procure food. A merchant certainly could not set out for South America or the East Indies unless he were confident that during the period of his absence he and his family could find subsistence, and that he would be able at the end of his voyage to pay all the expenses he had incurred. It is this assurance, this knowledge, this confidence of obtaining subsistence and reward, which enables and induces men to undertake long and complicated operations, and the question is, do men derive this assurance from a stock of goods already provided (saved from the produce of previous labour) and ready to pay them, or from any other source?

I shall endeavour to show that this assurance arises from a general principle in the constitution of Man, and that the effects attributed to a stock of commodities, under the name of circulating capital, are caused by co-existing labour.

The labourer, the real maker of any commodity, derives this assurance from a knowledge he has that the person who set him to work will pay him, and that with the money he will be able to buy what he requires. He is not in possession of any stock of commodities. Has the person who employs and pays him such a stock? Clearly not. Only a very few capitalists possess any of those commodities which the labourers they employ consume. Farmers may have a stock of corn, and merchants and shipowners may have a few weeks' or months' supply of provisions for their seamen, according to the length of the voyage they are to undertake; but, beyond this, no capitalist possesses ready prepared the commodities which his labourers require. He possesses money, he possesses credit with other capitalists, he possesses, under the sanction of the law, a power over the labour of the slave-descended labourer, but he does not possess food or clothing. He pays the labourer his money wages, and the expectation which other labourers have of receiving part of these wages or other wages, induces them in the meantime to prepare the clothing and food the labourer constantly requires. Not to deal, however, in general terms and abstractions, doing which seems to have led other writers astray, let us descend to particulars.

A great cotton manufacturer, we suppose, for example, a Sir Robert Peel, or any other of those leviathans who are so anxious to retain their power over us, and who, as legislators, either in their own persons or in the persons of their sons, make the laws which both calumniate and oppress us, employs a thousand persons, whom he pays weekly: does he possess the food and clothing ready prepared which these persons purchase and consume daily? Does he even know whether the food and clothing they receive are prepared and created? In fact, are the food and clothing which his labourers will consume prepared beforehand, or are other labourers busily employed in preparing food and clothing while his labourers are making cotton yarn? Do all the capitalists of Europe possess at this moment one week's food and clothing for all the labourers they employ?

Let us first examine the question as to food. One portion of the food of the people is **bread**, which is never prepared till within a few hours of the time when it is eaten. The corn of which the bread is made must, of course, have been grown, or one part of the whole operation, and that the longest part — that between saving the seed and harvesting the ripe grain, which is necessary to the complete preparation of the food, has been performed; but the corn has afterward to be thrashed, ground, sifted, brought to market and made into bread. For the cotton-spinner to be able to attend only to his peculiar species of industry, it is indispensable that other men should be constantly engaged in completing this complicated process, every part of it being as necessary as the part performed by the agriculturist. The produce of several of the labourers particularly of the baker, cannot be stored up. In no case can the material of bread, whether it exist as corn or flour, be preserved without continual labour. The employer of the working cotton-spinner can have no bread stored up, for there is none prepared; the labouring cotton-spinner himself knows nothing of any stock of corn being in existence from which his bread can be made; he knows that he has always been able to get bread when he had wherewithal to buy it, and further he does not require to know. But even if he did know of such a stock, he would probably give up cotton-spinning and take to preparing food, if he did not also know that while he is making cotton other labourers will till the ground, and prepare him food, which he will be able to procure by making cotton. His conviction that he will obtain bread when he requires it, and his master's conviction that the money he pays will enable him to obtain it, arise simply from the fact that the bread has always been obtained when required.

Another article of the labourer's food is milk, and milk is manufactured, not to speak irreverently of the operations of nature, twice a day. If it be said that the cattle to supply it are already there — why, the answer is, they require constant attention and constant labour, and their food, through the greater part of the year, is of daily growth. The fields in which they pasture require the hand of man; and, though some herds be drilled into the habits of obedience more perfect and certainly more pleasing to see than the obedience of soldiers, yet even they require perpetual attention, and their milk must be drawn from them twice a day. The meat, also, which the labourer eats is not ready, even for cooking, till it is on the shambles, and it cannot be stored up, for it begins instantly to deteriorate after it is brought to market. The cattle which are to be slaughtered require the same sort of care and attention as cows; and not one particle of meat could the cotton-spinner ever procure were not the farmer, the grazier and the drover continually at work, preparing meat while he is preparing cotton. But after the meat is brought to market, it is not even then ready for consumption. We are not cannibals; and either our wives, or some labourer who makes this his business, completes the preparation of the meat only a few hours, or even minutes, before it is eaten. Of the drink of the labourer, that which is supplied by nature never ceases to flow. His beer is prepared only so long before it is drunk as is necessary to have it good, and, while the existing stock is disposing of, the brewer is busy creating a fresh supply. There may probably be as much tea imported at one time as serves for a few months, and, while this stock is consuming, ships are continually arriving with more.

Now as to clothing. Some labourers buy ready-made clothes; others order them to be made for them. There is, it may be admitted, a small stock of clothing on hand; but considering what enemies moths are to the materials of which it is made, only a very small stock is ever prepared. The materials for women's garments may be prepared a few weeks before they are made up, but the garments are rarely formed till they are actually put on.

Other examples might be brought from every branch of industry, if it were necessary to examine each on in detail, for in this respect every labourer is similarly situated. The farmer knows he will be able to get clothes when he requires them, and the tailor knows he will be able to get food; but the former knows nothing of any stored-up stock of clothes, and the latter nothing of any stored-up stock of provisions. The labourer knows that when he is able to pay for bread, for meat and for drink he can procure them, but he knows nothing further; and I have shown that these are not prepared till he needs them. As far as food, drink and clothing are concerned, it is quite plain, then, that no species of labourer depends on any previously prepared stock, for in fact no such stock exists; but every species of labourer does constantly, and at all times, depend for his supplies on the co-existing labour of some other labourers.

To enable either the master manufacturer or the labourer to devote himself to any particular occupation, it is only necessary that he should possess — not, as political economists say, a stock of commodities, or circulating capital, but a conviction that while he is labouring at his particular occupation the things which he does not produce himself will be provided for him, and that he will be able to procure them and pay for them by the produce of his own labour. This conviction arises, in the first instance, without any reflection from habit. As we expect that the sun will rise tomorrow, so we also expect that men in all time to come will be actuated by the same motives as they have been in times past. If we push our inquiries still further, all that we can learn is, that there are other men in existence who are preparing those things we need, while we are preparing those which they need. The conviction may, perhaps, ultimately be traced them to our knowledge that other men exist and labour, but never to any conviction or knowledge that there is a stored-up stock of commodities. It is labour which produces all things as they are wanted, and the only thing which can be said to be stored up or previously prepared is the skill of the labourer. If the skill of the baker, butcher, grazier, tailor, weaver, etc., was not previously created and stored up, the commodities which each of them purchases could not be obtained; but where that skill exists, these commodities may always be procured when wanted.

We may suppose that the operation of cotton-spinning is completed, and the produce brought to market, so as to be exchanged or sold within a year; but there are many operations which are not completed within this period; and if it be true, as I have endeavoured to show, that there is not stock of food and clothing prepared, even for those labourers whose operations are completed within the period of two successive harvests, how much more evident must this truth be of those operations which are not completed within a year? All the labourers engaged in them have to rely on the baker, miller, butcher, etc., completing their part of the social task; and they must rely on the farmer, and that he will till his ground, and sow it, and reap the harvest of the following year. Mr Mill says and says justly, "what is annually produced is annually consumed." So that, in fact, to enable men to carry on all those operations which extend beyond a year there cannot be any stock of commodities stored up. Those who undertake them must rely, therefore, not on any commodities already created, but that other men will labour and produce what they are to subsist on till their own products are completed. Thus should the labourer admit that some accumulation of circulating capital is necessary for operations terminated within the year — and I have show how very limited that admission ought to be, if made at all — it is plain that in all operations which extend beyond a year the labourer does not, and he cannot, rely on accumulated capital.

The operations not terminated within the year are neither few nor unimportant. The time necessary to acquire a knowledge of any species of skilled labour, so as to practise it to advantage, which includes almost every art, whether it create wealth or merely contribute to amusement — the time necessary to perform all distant voyages, and construct most of the canals, roads, harbours, docks, large steam-engines and ships, all of which are afterward to be such powerful instruments in the hands of the labourer, is considerably more than a year, and is, in many cases, several years. All those who set about such undertakings have a practical conviction, though it is seldom expressed, that while they are teaching the rising generation skilled labour, and instructing their children in the useful arts, while they are making canals, roads, docks, ships, steam-engines, etc., that the farmer will continue to grow corn and the miller to grind it, that the baker will make it into bread, the grazier will fatten his cattle and the butcher slaughter them as they are needed, that the cotton and woollen manufacturers will go on preparing cloth and the tailor be always ready to make it up for them into clothes whenever it is ordered. Beyond this conviction they have nothing; they possess no stock of circulating capital themselves, nor do the persons who are afterwards to supply food and clothing during the whole time such undertakings are in progress possess any such stock at the moment when they are commenced.

Of all the important operations which require more than a year to complete them — and that they all are important, as far as the production of wealth is concerned, does not require to be asserted — by far the most important is the rearing of youth and teaching them skilled labour, or some wealth-creating art. I am particularly desirous of directing the reader's attention to this productive operation, because, if the observations I have already made be correct, all the effects usually attributed to accumulation of circulating capital are derived from the accumulation and storing up of skilled labour; and because this most important operation is performed, as far as the great mass of the labourers is concerned, without any circulating capital whatever. The labour of the parents produces and purchases, with what they receive as wages, all the food and the clothing which the rising generation of labourers use while they are learning those arts by means of which they will hereafter produce all the wealth of society. For the rearing and educating all future labourers (of course I do not mean book education, which is the smallest and least useful part of all which they have to learn) their parents have no stock stored up beyond their own practical skill. Under the strong influence of natural affection and parental love, they prepare by their toils, continued day after day, and year after year, through all the long period of the infancy and childhood of their offspring, those future labourers who are to succeed to their toils and their hard fare, but who will inherit their productive power, and be what they now are, the main pillars of the social edifice.

If we duly consider the number and importance of those wealth-producing operations which are not completed within the year, and the numberless products of daily labour, necessary to subsistence, which are consumed as soon as produced, we shall, I think, be sensible that the success and productive power of every different species of labour is at all times more dependent on the co-existing productive labour of other men than on any accumulation of circulating capital. The labourer, having no stock of commodities, undertakes to bring up his children, and teach them a useful art, always relying on his own labour; and various classes of persons undertake tasks the produce of which is not completed for a long period, relying on the labour of other men to procure them, in the meantime, what they require for subsistence. All classes of men carry on their daily toils in the full confidence that while each is engaged in his particular occupation some others will prepare whatever he requires, both for his immediate and future consumption and use. I have already explained that this confidence arises from that law of our nature by which we securely expect the sun will rise tomorrow, and that our fellow men will labour on the morrow and during the next year as they have laboured during the year and the day which have passed. I hope I have also satisfied the reader that there is no knowledge of any produce of previous labour stored up for use, that the effects usually attributed to a stock of commodities are caused by co-existing labour, and that it is by the command the capitalist possesses over the labour of some men, not by his possessing a stock of commodities, that he is enabled to support and consequently employ other labourers.

I come now to examine, secondly, the nature and effects of fixed capital. Fixed capital consists of the tools and instruments the labourer works with, the machinery he makes and guides, and the buildings he uses either to facilitate his exertions or to protect their produce. Unquestionably by using these instruments man adds wonderfully to his power. Without a hand saw, a portion of fixed capital, he could not cut a tree into planks; with such an instrument he could, though it would cost him many hours or days; but with a sawmill he could do it in a few minutes. Every man must admit that by means of instruments and machines the labourer can execute tasks he could not possibly perform without them; that he can perform a greater quantity of work in a given time, and that he can perform the work with greater nicety and accuracy than he could possibly do had he no instruments and machines. But the question then occurs, what produces instruments and machines, and in what degree do they aid production independent of the labourer, so that the owners of them are entitled to by far the greater part of the whole produce of the country? Are they, or are they not, the produce of labour? Do they, or do they not, constitute an efficient means of production, separate from labour? Are they, or are they not, so much inert decaying and dead matter, of no utility whatever, possessing no productive power whatever, but as they are guided, directed and applied by skilful hands? The reader will be able instantly to answer these questions, and I only add my answers because they lead to some conclusions different from those generally adopted.

It is admitted by those who contend most strenuously for the claims of capital that all instruments and machines are the produce of labour. They add, however, that they are the produce of previous labour, and are entitled to profit, on account of having been saved or stored up. But the manufacture of instruments and tools is quite as uninterrupted as the manufacture of food and clothing. They are not all consumed or used within a year, but they are brought into use as soon as possible after they are made. Nobody who manufactures them stores them up; nor does he make them for this purpose. As long as they are merely the result of previous labour, and are not applied to their respective uses by labourers, they do not repay the expense of making them. It is only when they are so applied that they bring any profit. They are made solely for the use of the labourer, and directly they come into his hands they return or repay the capitalist, the sum they cost him; and over and above this the labourer must give him an additional sum corresponding to the rate of profit in the country. It is plainly not the previous creation of these things which entitles them to profit, for most of them diminish in value from being kept. A man must pay also as much profit for the use of an instrument in proportion to the labour of making it, whether it be like sewing needles, of which many are used and made in the course of a week, or like a ship, or a steam engine, one of which lasts several years. Fixed capital does not derive its utility from previous, but present labour; and does not bring its owner a profit because it has been stored up, but because it is a means of obtaining a command over labour.

The production of fixed capital cannot be attributed to circulating capital, in the ordinary sense; but certainly those who make instruments must be confident they will be able to obtain food, or they would never think of making instruments. The smith, while he is making or mending the farmer's ploughshare, trusts to the farmer to do his part in procuring a supply of food; and the farmer, while he tills his fields, trusts to the smith to prepare for him the necessary instruments. These instruments are not the produce of circulating capital and of labour, but of labour alone, and of the labour of two or more co-existing persons. All fixed capital, not only in the first instance, as is generally admitted, but in every stage of society, at every period in the history of man, is the creation of labour and of skill, of different species of labour and skill certainly, but of nothing more than labour and skill.

After any instruments have been made, what do they effect? Nothing. On the contrary, they begin to rust or decay unless used or applied by labour. The most perfect instrument which the cunning hand of man can make is not instinct with life, and it constantly needs the directing hand of its creator, or of some other labourer. An artist may indeed make an automaton, or a timepiece, which will move for a certain period without further labour, but the motion he gives it is, in this case, the final object and aim of labour, and the instruments are not called fixed capital, because they are not used for further production. The automaton may be exhibited by its owner for money, and the timepiece, if employed to determine the longitude of a ship, may be a portion of fixed capital, useful in that production which is occasioned by commerce. In this case, however, there is an observer required, and it is by his labour and skill, he making use of the timepiece, that the ship's place is ascertained. Whether an instrument shall be regarded as productive capital or not depends entirely on its being used, or not, by some productive labourer.

The most perfect instruments ever made by labour require, as in the case of a timepiece, a peculiar skill to render them productive. A ship, for example, is undoubtedly a noble instrument, as admirable and useful a portion of fixed capital as the hand of man ever created, or his skill ever employed. By it the wealth of Great Britain has been and will be augmented. But our navy would lie and rot unless care were taken to preserve it; and the ships when turned adrift would be bruised by the waves, the winds or the rocks unless they were guided by seamen. By the skill acquired during many years' experience, and by much labour guided by this skill, a ship is built. It would trouble me to enumerate the various species of industry which are necessary to prepare her for sea. There is the skill and labour of the draughtsman, of the working shipwright, of the carpenter, the mast maker, the sail maker, the cooper, the founder, the smith, the coppersmith, the compass maker, etc., etc., but there is nothing necessary more than the skill and labour of these different persons. After she is made ready the same qualities watch over her, check the first indications of decay, and repair every little defect occasioned by accident and time. She is then, however, of no use unless there are seamen to manage her. To conduct her safely from port to port, and from hemisphere to hemisphere, a great deal of knowledge of the winds and tides, of the phenomena of the heavens, and of the laws which prevail on the surface of the earth, is necessary; and only when this knowledge is united with great skill, and carried into effect by labour, can a ship be safely conducted through the multitudes of dangers which beset her course. To have and to use this fixed capital, knowledge, labour and skill are necessary. Without these it could not be made, and when it would be less productive than the clod from which its materials spring, or from which they are fashioned by the hand of man.

A road is made by a certain quantity of labour, and is then called fixed capital; the constant repairs it needs, however, are a continual making, and the expense incurred by them is called circulating capital. But neither the circulating nor the fixed capital return any profit to the road makers unless there are persons to travel over the road or make a further use of their labour. The road facilitates the progress of the traveller, and just in proportion as people do travel over it, so does the labour which has been employed on the road become productive and useful. One easily comprehends why both these species of labour should be paid — why the road maker should receive some of the benefits accruing only to the road user; but I do not comprehend why all these benefits should go to the road itself and be appropriated by a set of person who neither make nor use it, under the name of profit for their capital. One is almost tempted to believe that capital is a sort of cabalistic word, like Church or State, or any other of those general terms which are invented by those who fleece the rest of mankind to conceal the hand that shears them. It is a sort of idol before which men are called upon to prostrate themselves, while the cunning priest from behind the altar, profaning the God whom he pretends to serve, and mocking those sweet sentiments of devotion and gratitude, or those terrible emotions of fear and resentment, one or the other of which seems common to the whole human race, as they are enlightened and wise, or ignorant and debased, puts forth his hand to receive and appropriate the offerings which he calls for in the name of religion.

A steam engine also is a most complete instrument, but alas! for the capitalist, it does not go of itself. A peculiar skill is required to make it and put it up, and peculiar skill and labour must afterwards direct and regulate its movements. What would it produce without the engineer? To the stranger who did not possess the engineer's skill, only misery, death and destruction. Its vast utility does not depend on stored up iron and wood, but on that practical and living knowledge of the powers of nature which enables some men to construct, and others to guide it.

If we descend to more minute instruments, and consider such as are guided by the hand, the necessity of skill and labour, and the utter worthlessness of capital by itself, will be still more obvious. It has been asked, what could a carpenter effect without his hatchet and his saw? I put the converse of the question, and ask what the hatchet and saw could effect without the carpenter. Rust and rottenness must be the answer. A plough or a scythe may be made with the most cunning art, but to use either of them a man must have a droit turn of the hand, or a peculiar species of skill. The shoemaker who can thrust awls through leather with singular dexterity and neatness cannot make any use of a watchmaker's tools; and the most skilful and dexterous maker of plane, saw and chisel blades would find it difficult to construct with them any of that furniture which the cabinet maker forms with so much dispatch and beautiful effect. Almost every species of workman, however, from having acquired a certain dexterity in the use of his hands, and from having frequently seen the operations of other workmen, could learn the art of another man much better than a person who had never practised any kind of manual dexterity, and never seen it practised. But if a skilled labourer could not direct any kind of instruments so well as the man who has been constantly accustomed to use them, it is plain that the whole productive power of such instruments must depend altogether on the peculiar skill of the artisan and mechanic, who has been trained to practise different arts. Fixed capital, of whatever species, then, is only a costly production, costly to make, and costly to preserve, without that particular species of skill and labour which guides each instrument, and which, as I have before shown, is nourished, instructed and maintained by wages alone.

The utility of the instruments the labourer uses can in no wise be separated from his skill. Whoever may be the owner of fixed capital — and in the present state of society he who makes it is not, and he who uses it is not — it is the hand and knowledge of the labourer which make it, preserve it from decay, and which use it to any beneficial end.

For a nation to have fixed capital, then, and to make a good use of it, three things, and only three things, seem to me to be requisite. First, knowledge and ingenuity for inventing machines. No labourer would, I am sure, be disposed to deny to these their reward. But no subject of complaint is more general or more just than that the inventor of any machine does not reap the benefit of it. Of all the immense number of persons who have acquired large fortunes by the modern improvements in steam engines and cotton mills, Mr Watt and Mr Arkwright are the only two, I believe, who have been distinguished for their inventions, they also acquired wealth less as inventors than as capitalists. Mr Watt found a capitalist who appreciated his genius, and Mr Arkwright saved and borrowed the means of profiting by his own inventions. Thousands of capitalist have been enriched by inventions and discoveries of which they were not the authors, and capital, by robbing the inventor of his just reward, is guilty of stifling genius. The second requisite for having fixed capital is the manual skill and dexterity for carrying these inventions into execution. The third requisite is the skill and labour to use these instruments after they are made. Without knowledge they could not be invented, without manual skill and dexterity they could not be made, and without skill and labour they could not be productively used. But there is nothing more than the knowledge, skill and labour requisite on which the capitalist can found a claim to any share of the produce.

Naturally and individually man is one of the most feeble and destitute of all created animals. His intelligence, however, compensates for his physical inferiority. After he has inherited the knowledge of several generations, and when he lives congregated into great masses, he is enabled by his mental faculties to complete, as it were, the work of nature, and add to his intelligence the physical powers of the lower animals. He directs his course on the waters, he floats in the air, he dives into the bowels of the earth, and all which its surface bears he makes tributary to his use. The gales which threaten at first to blow him from the earth, grind his corn, and waft to him a share in the treasures of the whole world. He creates at this pleasure the devouring element of fire, and checks its progress, so that it destroys only what he has no wish to preserve. He directs the course of the stream, and he sets bounds to the ocean; in short, he presses all the elements into his service, and makes Nature herself the handmaid to his will. The instruments he uses to do all this, which have been invented by his intelligence to aid his feeble powers, and which are employed by his skill and his hands, have been called fixed capital; and shutting out of view man himself, in order to justify the existing order of society, which is founded on property or possessions, and the existing oppression of the labourer, who forms unhappily part of these possessions — all these glorious effects have been attributed, with a more extraordinary perversion of thought, perhaps, than is to be found in any other department of knowledge, to fixed and circulating capital. The skill and the art of the labourer have been overlooked, and he has been vilified; while the work of his hands has been worshipped. 1

[1. In all errors which are generally adopted there is a tolerable substratum of truth. In the present case the substratum of truth is this: There was time in society when capital and capitalists were of the most essential service to it. On the establishment of towns in Europe, and on the introduction of manufactures into them, they became the refuge of all the oppressed and enslaved peasantry who could escape from their feudal tyrants. The capitalists and manufacturers who inhabited them were the skilled labourers, and really gave employment and protection to the peasantry. They taught them useful arts, and hence became invested with the character of benefactors, both to the poor and the state. They were infinitely better than the feudal barons with whom they were compared; and the character they then acquired they now retain. The veneration men have for capital and capitalists is founded on a sort of superstitious and transmitted notion of their utility in former times. But they have long since reduced the ancient tyrant of the soil to comparative insignificance, while they have inherited his power over all the labouring classes. It is, therefore, now time that the reproaches so long cast on the feudal aristocracy should be heaped on capital and capitalists; or on that still more oppressive aristocracy which is founded on wealth, and which is nourished by profit.]

I have now show the reader that the effects attributed to circulating capital result from co-existing labour, and the assurance common to each labourer, that he will be able to procure what he wants, or that while he is at work other men are also at work. I have also shown that fixed capital is produce by the skill of the labourer. Circulating capital, consisting of food and clothes, is created only for consumption; while fixed capital, consisting of instruments and tools, is made, not to be consumed, but to aid the labourer in producing those things which are to be consumed. There is no analogy between these two descriptions of commodities, except that both are the produce of labour, and both give the owner of them a profit.

There is, however, a striking difference between them which deserves to be noticed. It is usually stated that "the productive industry of any country is in proportion to its capital, increase when its capital increases, and declines when its capital declines." This position is true only of circulating capital, but not of fixed capital. The number of productive labourers depends certainly on the quantity of food, clothing, etc., produced and appropriated to their use; it is not, however, the quantity but the quality of the fixed capital on which the productive industry of a country depends. Instruments are productive, to use the improper language of the political economists, not in proportion as they multiplied, but as they are efficient. It is probable that since Mr Watt's improvements on the steam engine one man can perform as much work with these instruments as ten men did before. As the efficiency of the fixed capital is increased by men obtaining greater knowledge and greater skill, it is quite possible, and is the case, that a greater quantity of commodities, or a greater means of nourishing and supporting men, is obtained with less capital. Although, therefore, the number of labourers must at all times depend on the quantity of circulating capital, or, as I should say, on the quantity of the products of co-existing labour, which labourers are allowed to consume, the quality of commodities they produce will depend on the efficiency of their fixed capital. Circulating capital nourishes and supports men as its quantity is increased; fixed capital as a means of nourishing and supporting men depends for its efficiency altogether on the skill of the labourer, and consequently the productive industry of a country, as far as fixed capital is concerned, is in proportion to the knowledge and skill of the people.

The warmest admirers of circulating capital will not pretend that it adds in the same way as fixed capital to the productive power of the labourer. The most extraordinary visionary who ever wrote cannot suppose circulating capital adds anything to productive power. The degree and nature of the utility of both species of capital is perfectly different and distinct. The labourer subsists on what is called circulating capital; he works with fixed capital. But equal quantities or equal values of both these species of capital bring their owner precisely the same amount of profit. We may, from this single circumstance, be quite sure that the share claimed by the capitalist for the use of fixed capital is not derived from the instruments increasing the efficiency of labour, or from the utility of these instruments; and profit is derived in both cases from the power which the capitalist has over the labourer who consumes the circulating, and who uses the fixed, capital. How he obtained this power I shall not now inquire, further than to state that it is derived from the whole surface of the country, having been at one period monopolised by a few persons; and the consequent state of slavery in which the labourer formerly existed in this country, as well as throughout Europe. As the profits of the capitalist on fixed capital are not derived from the utility of these instruments, it is useless to inquire what share ought to belong to the owner of the wood and iron, and what share ought to belong to the person who uses them. He who makes the instruments is entitled, in the eye of justice, and in proportion to the labour he employs, to as great a reward as he who uses them; but he is not entitled to a greater; and he who neither makes nor uses them has no just claim to any portion of the produce.

Betwixt him who produces food and him who produces clothing, betwixt him who makes instruments and him who uses them, in steps the capitalist, who neither makes nor uses them, and appropriates to himself the produce of both. With as niggard a hand as possible he transfers to each a part of the produce of the other, keeping to himself the large share. Gradually and successively has he insinuated himself betwixt them, expanding in bulk as he has been nourished by their increasingly productive labours, and separating them so widely from each other that neither can see whence that supply is drawn which each receives through the capitalist. While he despoils both, so completely does he exclude one from the view of the other that both believe they are indebted him for subsistence. He is the middleman of all labourers; and when we compare what the skilled labour of England produces, with the produce of the untutored labour of the Irish peasantry, the middlemen of England cannot be considered as inferior in their exactions to the middlemen of Ireland. They have been more fortunate, however, and while the latter are stigmatised as oppressors, the former are honoured as benefactors. Not only do they appropriate the produce of the labourer; but they have succeeded in persuading him that they are his benefactors and employers. At least such are the doctrines of political economy; and capitalist may well be pleased with a science which both justifies their claims and holds them up to our admiration, as the great means of civilising and improving the world.

To show the labourer the effects which bestowing this abundant reward on the supposed productive powers of food, clothing and instruments have on his poverty or wealth, I must observe that all political economists agree in saying that all savings in society are usually made by capitalists. The labourer cannot save; the landlord is not disposed to save; whatever is saved is saved from profits and becomes the property of the capitalists. Now let us suppose that a capitalist possesses, when profit is at ten per cent per annum, 100 quarters of wheat and 100 steam engines; he must at the end of a year be paid for allowing the labourer to eat this wheat and use these steam engines with 110 quarters of wheat and 110 steam engines, all in the same excellent condition as the 100 steam engines were at the beginning. It being an admitted principle that, after a portion of fixed capital is prepared, it must be paid for at a rate sufficient to pay the ordinary rate of interest, and provide for the repairs or the remaking of the instrument. Let us suppose that 5 quarters of wheat and 5 steam engines, or the value of this quantity, suffices for the owner's consumption, and that the other 5 of his profit being added to this capital he has the next year 105 quarters of wheat and 105 steam engines, which he allows labourers to eat or use; for these the labourer must produce for him, the following year, supposing the rate of profit to continue the same, a sufficient sum to replace the whole of this capital, with the interest, or 115 quarters 4 bushels of wheat and 155 1/2 steam engines. Supposing that the value of the 5 quarters and of 5 steam engines suffices for the consumption of the capitalist, he will have the next year 110 quarters 4 bushels, and 110 1/2 steam engines, for the use of which he must be paid at the same rate; or the labourer must produce and give him, the third year, 121 quarters and 1/20th of a quarter, and 121 steam engines and 1/20th of a steam engine. It is of no use calculating all these fractions, or carrying the series further; it is enough to observe that every atom of the capitalist's revenue, which he puts out to use, or, as it is called, saves, which means given or lent to labourers, goes on increasing at compound interest. Dr Price has calculated that the sum of one penny put out to compound interest at our Saviour's birth, at 5 per cent, would in the year 1791 amount to a sum greater than could be contained in three hundred millions of globes like this earth, all solid gold.

Perhaps I can make the evil effects of capital more apparent by another sort of example. The real price of a coat or a pair of shoes or a loaf of bread, all which nature demands from man in order that he may have either of these very useful articles, is a certain quantity of labour; how much it is almost impossible to say, from the manufacture of a coat, a pair of shoes or a loaf of bread being completed by many persons. But for the labourer to have either of these articles he must give over and above the quantity of labour nature demands from him, a still large quantity to the capitalist. Before he can have a coat, he must pay interest for the farmer's sheep, interest on the wool after it has got into the hands of the wool merchant, interest for this same wool as raw material, after it is in the hands of the manufacturer, interest on all buildings and tools he uses, and interest on all the wages he pays his men. Moreover, he must pay interest or profit on the tailor's stock, both fixed and circulating, and this rate of interest is increased in all these instances by something more being always necessary to pay the rent of all these different capitalists. In the same manner before a labourer can have a loaf of bread he must give a quantity of labour more than the loaf costs, by all that quantity which pays the profit of the farmer, the corn dealer, the miller and the baker, with profit on all the buildings they use; and he must, moreover, pay with the produce of his labour the rent of the landlord. How much more labour a labourer must give to have a loaf of bread than that loaf costs, it is impossible for me to say. I should probably underrate it were I to state it at six times; or were I to say that the real cost of that loaf, for which the labourer must give sixpence, is one penny. Of this, however, I am quite certain, that the Corn Laws, execrable as they are in principle, and mischievous as they are to the whole community, do not impose anything like so heavy a tax on the labourer as capital. Indeed, however injurious they may be to the capitalist, it may be doubted whether they are so to the labourer. They diminish the rate of profit, but they do not in the end lower the wages of labour. Whether there are Corn Laws or not, the capitalist must allow the labourer to subsist, and as long as his claims are granted and acted on he will never allow him to do more. In other words, the labourer will always have to give much about the same quantity of labour to the capitalist for a loaf, whether that loaf be the produce of one hour's or one day's labour. Knowing the vast influence capitalists have in society, one is not surprised at the anathemas which have of late been hurled against the Corn Laws, nor at the silence which has been preserved with respect to their more mighty and, to the labourer, more mischievous exactions.

What the capitalist really puts out to interest, however, is not gold or money, but food, clothing and instruments; and his demand is always to have more food, clothing and instruments produced than he puts out. No productive power can answer this demand, and both the capitalists and political economists find fault with the wisdom of Nature, because she refuses to minister to the avarice of the former, and does not exactly square in her proceedings with the wishes of the latter.

Of course the ultimate term to which compound interest tends can never be reached. Its progress is gradually but perpetually checked, and it is obliged to stop far short of the desired goal. Accordingly, in most books on Political Economy, one or the other of two causes is assigned for the constant falling off of profit in the progress of society. The political economists either say, with Adam Smith, that the accumulation of capital lowers profits, or, with Mr Ricardo, that profits are lowered by the increasing difficulty of procuring subsistence. Neither of them has assigned it to the right cause, the impossibility of the labourer answering the demands of the capitalist. A mere glance must satisfy every mind that simple profit does not decrease but increase in the progress of society

— that is, the same quantity of labour which at any former period produced 100 quarters of wheat and 100 steam engines will now produce somewhat more, or the value of somewhat more, which the same thing: or where is the utility of all our boasted improvements? In fact, also, we find that a much greater number of persons now live in opulence on profit in this country than formerly.

It is clear, however, that no labour, no productive power, no ingenuity and no art can answer the overwhelming demands of compound interest. But all saving is made from the revenue of the capitalist, so that actually these demands are constantly made, and as constantly the productive power of labour refuse to satisfy them. A sort of balance is, therefore, constantly struck. The capitalists permit the labourers to have the means of subsistence because they cannot do without labour, contenting themselves very generously with taking every particle of produce not necessary to this purpose. It is the overwhelming nature of the demands of capital sanctioned by the laws of society, sanctioned by the customs of men, enforced by the legislature, and warmly defended by political economists, which keep, which every have kept, and which ever will keep, as long as they are allowed and acquiesced in, the labourer in poverty and misery.

It is the overwhelming and all-engrossing nature of compound interest, also, which gives to Mr Ricardo's theory and his definitions, as I have already described them, though this principle is nowhere brought sufficiently into view in his book, their mathematical accuracy and truth. I refer to them, not as caring much to illustrate the subtleties of that ingenious and profound writer, but because his theory confirms the observations I have just made — viz. that the exactions of the capitalist cause the poverty of the labourer. It is an admitted principle that there cannot be two rates of profit in a country, and therefore the capital of the man who cultivates the best soil of a country procures of its owner no more than the capital of the man who cultivates the worst soil. The superior produce of the best soil is not, therefore, profit, and Mr Ricardo has called it rent. It is a portion of produce over and above the average rate of profit, and Mr Ricardo has assigned it to the landlords. The labourer must, however, live, though the exorbitant claims of capital allow him only a bare subsistence. Mr Ricardo has also been aware of this, and has therefore justly defined the price of labour to be such a quantity of commodities as will enable the labourers, one with another, to subsist, and to perpetuate their race without either increase or diminution. Such is all which the nature of profit or interest on capital will allow them to receive, and such has ever been their reward. The capitalist must give the labourers this sum, for it is the condition he must fulfil in order to obtain labourers; it is the limit which nature places to his claims, but he will never give, and never has given, more. The capitalists, according to Mr Ricardo's theory, allow the landlords to have just as much as keeps all the capitalist on a level; the labourers they allow, in the same theory, barely to subsist. Thus Mr Ricardo would admit that the cause of the poverty of the labourer is the engrossing nature of compound interest; this keeps him poor, and prevents him from obeying the commands of his Creator, to increase and multiply.

Though the defective nature of the claims of capital may now be satisfactorily proved, the question as to the wages of labour is by no means decided. Political economists, indeed, who have insisted very strongly on the necessity of giving security to property, and have ably demonstrated how much that security promotes general happiness, will not hesitate to agree with me when I say that whatever labour produces ought to belong to it. They have always embraced the maxim of permitting those to "reap who sow," and they have maintained that the labour of a man's body and the work of his hands are to be considered as exclusively his own. I take it for granted, therefore, that they will henceforth maintain that the whole produce of labour ought to belong to the labourer. But though this, as a general proposition, is quite evident, and quite true, there is a difficulty, in its practical application, which no individual can surmount. There is no principle or rule, as far as I know, for dividing the produce of joint labour among the different individuals who concur in production, but the judgment of the individuals themselves; that judgment depending on the value men may set on different species of labour can never be known, nor can any rule be given for its application by any single person. As well might a man say what others shall hate or what they shall like.

Whatever division of labour exists, and the further it is carried the more evident does this truth become, scarcely any individual completes of himself any species of produce. Almost any product of art and skill is the result of joint and combined labour. So dependent is man on man, and so much does this dependence increase as society advances, that hardly any labour of any single individual, however much it may contribute to the whole produce of society, is of the least value but as forming a part of the great social task. In the manufacture of a piece of cloth, the spinner, the weaver, the bleacher and the dyer are all different persons. All of them except the first is dependent for his supply of materials on him, and of what use would his thread be unless the others took it from him, and each performed that part of the task which is necessary to complete the cloth? Wherever the spinner purchases the cotton or wool, the price which he can obtain for his thread, over and above what he paid for the raw material, is the reward of his labour. But it is quite plain that the sum the weaver will be disposed to give for the thread will depend on his view of its utility. Wherever the division of labour is introduced, therefore, the judgment of other men intervenes before the labourer can realise his earnings, and there is no longer any thing which we can call the natural reward of individual labour. Each labourer produces only some part of a whole, and each part having no value or utility of itself, there is nothing on which the labourer can seize, and say: "This is my product, this will I keep to myself." Between the commencement of any joint operation, such as that of making cloth, and the division of its product among the different persons whose combined exertions have produced it, the judgment of men must intervene several times, and the question is, how much of this joint product should go to each of the individuals whose united labourers produce it?

I know no way of deciding this but by leaving it to be settled by the unfettered judgments of the labourers themselves. If all kinds of labour were perfectly free, if no unfounded prejudice invested some parts, and perhaps the least useful, of the social task with great honour, while other parts are very improperly branded with disgrace, there would be no difficulty on this point, and the wages of individual labour would be justly settled by what Dr Smith calls the "higgling of the market." Unfortunately, labour is not, in general, free; and, unfortunately there are a number of prejudices which decree very different rewards to different species of labour from those which each of them merits.

Unfortunately, also, there is, I think, in general, a disposition to restrict the term labour to the operation of the hands. But if it should be said that the skill of the practised labourer is a mere mechanical sort of thing, nobody will deny that the labour by which he acquired that skill was a mental exertion. The exercise of that skill also, as it seems to me, requiring the constant application of judgment, depends much more on a mental than on a bodily acquirement. Probably the mere capacity of muscular exertion is as great, or greater, among a tribe of Indians as among the most productive Europeans; and the superior productive power of Europeans, and of one nation over another, arise from the different nature of their fixed capital. But I have shown that the greater efficacy of fixed capital depends on the skill of the labourer; so that we come to the conclusion that not mere labour, but mental skill, or the mode in which labour is directed, determines its productive powers. I therefore would caution my fellow labourers not to limit the term labour to the operations of the hands.

Before many of our most useful machines and

instruments could be invented, a vast deal of knowledge gathered in the progress of the world by many generations was necessary. At present also a great number of persons possessed of different kinds of knowledge and skill must combine and cooperate, although they have never entered into any express contract for this purpose, before many of our most powerful machines can be completed and before thy can be used. The labour of the draughtsman is as necessary to construct a ship as the labour of the man who fastens her planks together. The labour of the engineer, who "in his mind's eye" sees the effect of every contrivance, and who adapts the parts of a complicated machine to each other, is as necessary to the completion of that machine as the man who casts or fits any part of it, without being sensible of the purpose for which the whole is to serve. In like manner the labour and the knowledge of many different persons must be combined before almost any product intended for consumption can be brought to market. The knowledge and skill of the master manufacturer, or of the man who plans and arranges a productive operation, who must know the state of the markets and the qualities of different materials, and who has some tact in buying and selling, are just as necessary for the complete success of any complicated operation as the skill of the workmen whose hands actually alter the shape and fashion of these materials. Far be it, therefore, from the manual labourer, while he claims the reward due to his own productive powers, to deny its appropriate reward to any other species of labour, whether it be of the head or the hands. The labour and skill of the contriver, or of the man who arranges an adapts a whole, are as necessary as the labour and skill of him who executes only a part, and they must be paid accordingly.

    I must, however, add that it is doubtful whether one species of labour is more valuable than another; certainly it is not more necessary. But because those who have been masters. Planners, contrivers, etc., have in general also been capitalists, and have also had a command over the labour of those who have worked with their hands, their labour has been paid as much too high as common labour has been under paid. The wages of the master, employer or contriver has been blended with the profit of the capitalists, and he may probably be still disposed to claim the whole as only the proper reward of his exertions. On the other hand, manual labourers, oppressed by the capitalist, have never been paid high enough, and even now are more disposed to estimate their own deserts rather by what they have hitherto received than by what they produce. This sort of prejudice makes it, and will long make it, difficult even for labourers themselves to apportion with justice the social reward or wages of each individual labourer. No statesman can accomplish this, nor ought the labourers to allow any statesman to interfere in it. The labour is theirs, the produce ought to be theirs, and they alone ought to decide how much each deserves of the produce all. While each labourer claims his own reward, let him cheerfully allow the just claims of every other labourer; but let him never assent to the strange doctrine that the food he eats and the instruments he uses, which are the work of his own hands, become endowed, by merely changing proprietors, with productive power greater than his, and that the owner of them is entitled to a more abundant reward than the labour, skill and knowledge which produce and use them.

Masters, it is evident, are labourers as well as their journeymen. In this character their interest is precisely the same as that of their men. But they are also either capitalist, or the agents of the capitalist, and in this respect their interest is decidedly opposed to the interest of their workmen. As the contrivers and enterprising undertakers of new works, they may be called employers as well as labourers, and they deserve the respect of the labourer. As capitalist, and as the agents of he capitalist, they are merely middlemen, oppressing the labourer, and deserving of anything but his respect. The labourer should know and bear this in mind. Other people should also remember it, for it is indispensable to correct reasoning to distinguish between these two characters of all masters. If by combining the journeymen were to drive masters, who are a useful class of labourers, out of the country, if they were to force abroad the skill and ingenuity which contrive, severing them from the hands which execute, they would do themselves and the remaining inhabitants considerable mischief. If, on the contrary, by combining they merely incapacitate the masters from obtaining any profit on their capital, and merely prevent them from completing the engagements they have contracted with the capitalist, they will do themselves and the country incalculable service. They may reduce or destroy altogether the profit of the idle capitalist — and from the manner in which capitalists have treated labourers, even within our own recollection, they have no claim on the gratitude of the labourer — but they will augment the wages and rewards of industry, and will give to genius and skill their due share of the national produce. They will also increase prodigiously the productive power of the country by increasing the number of skilled labourers. The most successful and widest spread possible combination to obtain an augmentation of wages would have no other injurious effect than to reduce the incomes of those who live on profit and interest, and who have no just claim but custom to any share of the national produce.

It has indeed been said by some sapient legislators, both Lords and Commoners, that the journeymen will do themselves incalculable mischief by driving capital out of the country; and one of the reasons urged for the new law was that it would prevent the journeymen injuring themselves. Whenever the devil wants to do mischief he assumes the garb of holiness, and whenever a certain class of persons wish to commit a more than usually flagrant violation of justice it is always done in the name of humanity. If the labourers are disposed blindly to injure themselves I see no reason for the legislature interfering to prevent them; except as a farmer watches over the health of his cattle, or a West India planter looks after the negroes because they are his property, and bring him a large profit. The journeymen, however, know their own interest better than it is known to the legislator; and they would be all the richer if there were not an idle capitalist in the country. I shall not enter into any investigation of the origin of this opinion that the workmen will injure themselves by driving away capital; but it would not be difficult to show that it springs from the false theory I have opposed, and that it is based on a narrow experience. Because there are a few instances of political and religious persecution, driving both masters and journeymen, or a large quantity of national stock of skilled labour, from different countries, greatly, I admit, to the injury, and justly so, of the remaining inhabitants who permitted or practised this persecution, it has been asserted that this injury was caused by the banishment, not of the men but of the capital; and it being, therefore, now concluded that the proceedings of the workmen will in like manner banish capital from this country it has been affirmed that they will injure both themselves and the rest of the inhabitants. But they carry on neither political nor religious persecution, and it is somewhat preposterous in the race of politicians, by way, perhaps, of throwing a veil over their own crimes, to attribute to the actions of the workmen the same consequences as have been produced by some of the absurd and cruel proceedings of their own class. If the workmen do not frighten away the skill of the contriver and the master — and where can that be put to so good a use as where there are plenty of skilful hands — and even if they should, the wide spread of education among the mechanics and artisans will soon repair the loss, they will frighten away no other part of the national advantages. The merest tyro in political economy knows that the capitalist cannot export any great quantity of food, clothing and machines from this country, nor even the gold and silver which forms the current coin of the realm, to any advantage; either he must bring back an equivalent, which returns him a profit when consumed here, or he must carry with him those skilled labourers who have hitherto produced him his profit as they have consumed his food and used his instruments and machines. There is not a political injury on the one hand and both masters and workmen on the other; but on the one side is the labourer and on the other the capitalist, and however successful the workmen may be, the smallest fraction of their produce which the capitalist can scrape up he will assuredly stay to collect. The combination of the workmen will not frighten away their own skill, nor unlearn them what thy have learned. Their hand will not forget its cunning, when its produce goes no longer into the pocket of the capitalist. Capitalists, who can grow rich only where there is an oppressed body of labourers, may probably carry off some of their cloth, and their corn, and their machines to some country like Prussia, where the poor people can learn nothing but what the king and his schoolmasters please; or like France, where a watchful police allows no man to utter a thought but such as suits the views of a government and priesthood anxious to restore despotism and superstition; but they cannot, unless the labourers please, carry with them the mouths which consume, or the hands which make their capital useful; and where these are there will be the productive power. Our labourers already possess in an eminent degree the skill to execute, and they are rapidly acquiring also the skill to contrive. Never was there a more idle threat uttered, therefore, than that the combinations of skilled labourers to obtain greater rewards than they now possess will drive skilled labour from the country.

This analysis also of the operations of capital leads us at once boldly to pronounce all those schemes of which we have of late heard so much for improving countries, by sending capital to them, to be mere nonsense. Of what use, for example, would the butter and salt beef and pork and grain now exported from Ireland be of in that country if they were to be left there, or if they were to be sent back? All these articles form some of the most valuable parts of circulating capital, and so far from there being any want of them in Ireland, they are constantly exported in great quantities. It is plain, therefore, that there is no want of circulating capital in Ireland, if the capitalist would allow the wretched producer of it to consume it. Of what use also would steam engines or power looms or stocking frames or mining tools be to the ragged peasantry of Ireland? Of none whatever.

If, indeed, masters and journeymen went over with these instruments and tools, they might use them, and by consuming at the same time the circulating capital now exported from Ireland give the owner of it a large profit; and they might teach the ignorant and helpless natives how to make use of the various instruments I have mentioned. Those who talk of improving Ireland, or any other country, by capital have a double meaning in their words. They know the power of the capitalist over the labourer, and that whenever the master goes or sends, there also must the slave labourer go. But neither the law-maker nor the capitalist possesses any miraculous power of multiplying loaves and fishes; or of commanding, like the enchanters of old, broomsticks to do the work of men. They must have labourers, skilled labourers, and without them it is nonsense to talk of improving a country and a people by corn and cloth and hatchets and saws.

The wide spread of education among the journeyman mechanics of this country diminishes daily the value of the labour and skill of almost all masters and employers by increasing the number of persons who possess their peculiar knowledge. At the same time, masters and employers cannot hope that the labourers who are not capitalists will remain long ignorant of the manner in which masters who are both labourers and capitalist lend themselves to the views of the capitalists who are not labourers. They are daily acquiring this knowledge, and masters cannot therefore rationally expect a termination to the present contest. On the contrary, it must continue. Even if it should be stopped, it will again and again occur. It is not possible that any large body of men who are acquainted with their rights will tacitly acquiesce in insult and injury. The profits of the masters, as capitalist, must be diminished, whether the labourers succeed in obtaining higher wages, or the combination continues, or it is from time to time renewed. In the former case, the masters, as skilled labourers, will share in the increased rewards of industry; in either of the two latter, not only will their profit be destroyed, but their wages will be diminished or altogether annihilated. Without workmen their own skill and labour are of no use, but they may live in comfort and opulence without the capitalist. Masters and employers, therefore, would do well to recollect that by supporting the claims of capital they diminish their own wages, and they prolong a contest which, independent of the ill temper and hatred it creates and perpetuates, is also injurious to them as inventors, contrivers and skilled labourers, and which must ultimately terminate to their disadvantage.

The improved education of the labouring classes ought, in the present question, to have great weight also with statesmen, and with the community at large. The schools, which are everywhere established, or are establishing, for their instruction, make it impossible for the greatest visionary to suppose that any class of men can much longer be kept in ignorance of the principles on which societies are formed and governed. Mechanics' institutions will teach men the moral as well as the physical sciences. They excite a disposition to probe all things to the bottom, and supply the means of carrying research into every branch of knowledge. He must be a very blind statesman who does not see in this indications of a more extensive change in the frame of society than has ever yet been made. This change will not be effected by violence, and cannot be counteracted by force. Holy Alliance can put down the quiet insurrection by which knowledge will subvert whatever is not founded in justice and truth. The interest of the different classes of labourers who are now first beginning to think and act as a body, in opposition to the other classes among whom, with themselves, the produce of the earth is distributed, and who are now only for the first time beginning to acquire as extensive a knowledge of the principles of government as those who rule, is too deeply implicated by these principles to allow them to stop short in their career of inquiry. They may care nothing about the curious researches of the geologist or the elaborate classification of the botanist, but they will assuredly ascertain why they only of all classes of society have always been involved in poverty and distress. They will not stop short of any ultimate truth; and they have experienced too few of the advantages of society to make them feel satisfied with the present order of things. The mind is rather invigorated than enfeebled by the labour of the hands; and they will carry forward their investigations undelayed by the pedantry of learning, and undiverted by the fastidiousness of taste. By casting aside the prejudices which fetter the minds of those who have benefited by their degradation, they have everything to hope. On the other hand, they are the suffers by these prejudices, and have everything to dread from their continuance. Having no reason to love those institutions which limit the reward of labour, whatever may be its produce, to a bare subsistence, they will not spare them, whenever they see the hollowness of the claims made on their respect. As the labourers acquire knowledge, the foundations of the social edifice will be dug up from the deep beds into which they were laid in times past, they will be curiously handled and closely examined, and they will not be restored unless they were originally laid in justice, and unless justice commands their preservation.

Without joining in any of the commonplace observations against taking interest, and against usury, which, however, support my view of capital, I have show that it has no just claim to any share of the labourer's produce, and that what it actually receives is the cause of the poverty of the labourer. It is impossible that the labourer should long remain ignorant of these facts, or acquiesce in this state of things.

In truth, also, however the matter may be disguised, the combinations among workmen to obtain higher wages, which are now so general and so much complained of, are practical attacks on the claims of capital. The weight of its chains are felt, though the hand may not yet be clearly seen which imposes them. Gradually as the resistance increases, as laws are multiplied for the protection of capital, as claims for higher wages shall be more strenuously and more violently repressed, the cause of this oppression will be more distinctly seen. The contest now appears to be between masters and journeymen, or between one species of labour and another, but it will soon be displayed in its proper characters; and will stand confessed a war of honest industry against the idle profligacy which has so long ruled the affairs of the political world with undisputed authority — which has, for its own security, added honour and political power to wealth, and has conjoined exclusion and disgrace with the poverty it has inflicted on the labourer. On the side of the labourers there is physical strength, for they are more numerous than their opponents. They are also fast losing that reverence for their opponents which was and is the source of their power, and they are daily acquiring a moral strength which results from a common interest and a close and intimate union.

The capitalist and labourers form the great majority of the nation, so that there is not third power to intervene betwixt them. The must and will decide the dispute of themselves. Final success, I would fain hope, must be on the side of justice. I am certain, however, that till the triumph of labour be complete; till productive industry alone be opulent, and till idleness alone be poor, till the admirable maxim that "he who sows shall reap" be solidly established; till the right of property shall be founded on principles of justice, and not on those of slavery; till man shall be held more in honour than the clod be treads on, or the machine he guides — there cannot, and there ought not to be either peace on earth or goodwill amongst men.

Those who of late have shown themselves so ready to resist the just claims of labour, who, under the influence of interest and passion, have hurried into the arena with their penal laws, and have come forward, brandishing their parchment statutes, as if they, poor beings, could whip mankind into patience and submission, when these weapons of theirs — these penal laws and parchment statutes — derive all their power, whether for evil or for good, from the sanctity with which we are pleased to invest them, and as if they also did not know that they are as powerless as the meanest individual whom they are so prompt to scourge, except as we are pleased to submit and to honour them — they may thank themselves should their haste and their violence beget a corresponding haste and violence in others; and, should the labourers, who have hitherto shown themselves confiding and submissive — losing that reverence by which laws are invested with power, and to which Government is indebted for its existence — turn their attention from combining for higher wages, to amending the state, and to subverting a system which they must now believe is intended only to support all the oppressive exactions of capital. Ministers are undoubtedly, for the moment, very popular, but it does not require any very enlarged view to predict that by openly committing the Government during the last session of Parliament, when the great mass of the community are able both to scan the motives of their conduct and its consequences, and zealous in doing it, to a contest between capital and labour, taking the side of idleness against industry, of weakness against strength, of oppression against justice, they are preparing more future mischief than any ministry this country has ever seen. They profess liberal principles — and they make laws to keep the labourer in thraldom. By their innovations they encourage inquiry, and convince us the system is neither sacred nor incapable of improvement. They have practically told the labourer there is nothing deserving his reverence, and have excited his hostility both by insult and oppression.

 I do not mean, on the present occasion, to point out all the consequences which result from this view of capital, but there is one so important in a theoretical point of view, and so well calculated to relieve the wise system of the universe from the opprobrium which has been cast upon it in these latter times, that I cannot wholly pass it by. An elaborate theory has been constructed to show that there is a natural tendency in population to increase faster than capital, or than the means of employing labour. In Mr Mill's Elements of Political Economy, a work distinguished by its brevity, several sections and pages are devoted merely to announce this truth. If my view of capital be correct, this, as a theory of nature, falls at once baseless to the ground. That the capitalist can control the existence and number of labourers, that the whole number of the population depends altogether on him, I will not deny. But put the capitalist, the oppressive middleman, who eats up the produce of labour and prevents the labourer from knowing on what natural laws his existence and happiness depend, out of view — put aside those social regulations by which they who produce all are allowed to own little or nothing — and it is plain that capital, or the power to employ labour, and co-exiting labour are one; and that productive capital and skilled labour are also one; consequently capital and a labouring population are precisely synonymous.

In the system of nature, mouths are united with hands and with intelligence; they and not capital are the agents of production; and, according other rule, however it may have been thwarted by the pretended wisdom of law makers, wherever there is a man there also are the means of creating or producing him subsistence. If also, as I say, circulating capital is only co-existing labour, and fixed capital only skill labour, it must be plain that all those numerous advantages, those benefits to civilisation, those vast improvements in the condition of the human race, which have been in general attributed to capital, are caused in fact by labour, and by knowledge and skill informing and directing labour. Should it be said, then, as perhaps it may, that unless there be profit, and unless there be interest, there will be no motives for accumulation and improvement, I answer that this is a false view, and arises from attributing to capital and saving those effects which result from labour; and that the best means of securing the progressive improvement, both of individuals and of nations, is to do justice, and allow labour to possess and enjoy the whole of its produce.

Also available from the publisher:

A Discourse of Trade – Nicholas Barbon

Selected Works of Salvador Allende

Ethics of Socialism – Ernest Belfort Bax

Twenty Years in Underground Russia – Cecilia Bobrovskaya

The Decline of American Capitalism – Lewis Corey

Imperialism and the Revolution – Enver Hoxha

The Selected Works of Kim Il Sung

The Stalin Era – Anna Louise Strong

Three Lectures on the Rate of Wages – Nassau Senior

Principles of Philosophy of the Future – Ludwig Feuerbach

www.PrismKeyPress.com

www.ingramcontent.com/pod-product-compliance
Lightning Source LLC
Chambersburg PA
CBHW071642170526
45166CB00003B/1403